365 Anonymous Quotes Journal

Your Daily Dose of Encouraging & Entertaining Thoughts Throughout the Year

QUOTES COMPILED BY

MELISSA ALVAREZ

Published by

Adrema Press

Published by Adrema Press 2023

ISBN: 978-1-59611-148-6

Cover Design by Melissa Alvarez at https://BookCovers.us

All quotes in this book are of unknown origin and are therefore in the public domain and available to be used without permission or attribution to any person other than "Anonymous".

OTHER BOOKS BY MELISSA ALVAREZ

365 Ways to Raise Your Frequency
365 Days to Raise Your Frequency Journal
Llewellyn's Little Book of Spirit Animals
Earth Frequency
Earth Frequency Journal
Your Psychic Self
My Psychic Journal
Animal Frequency®
Animal Frequency® Journal
Animal Frequency® Oracle Cards
The Spirituality of Coziness
The Spirituality of Coziness Journal
Believe and Receive
Believe and Receive Journal
Believe and Receive Mini Meditation Cards
Simply Give Thanks
Simply Give Thanks Gratitude Journal
Chakra Divination® Card & Charts Activity Book
Chakra Divination® Ultimate Balance Journal
The Essential Guide to Chakra Divination®
Chakra Divination® Card Deck
The Phoenix's Guide to Self-Renewal
Your Color Power
Analyze Your Handwriting
Ghosts, A Spirit Guide and A Past Life
Paranormal Investigative Groups Around the World

WRITING AS ARIANA DUPRE

Night Visions
Talgorian Prophecy
Talgorian Dragon
Briar Mountain
Paradise Designs
Paranormal Adventures

And many more...
Please visit http://MelissaA.com for the complete booklist.

About the Author

Melissa Alvarez is a bestselling author, editor, and book cover designer who has written thirty-two books, novels, short stories, and mind/body/spirit nonfiction titles as well as nearly 500 articles on self-help, spirituality, and wellness. As a professional intuitive coach, energy worker, spiritual advisor, medium, and animal communicator with over 35 years of experience, Melissa has helped thousands of people bring clarity, joy, and balance into their lives. Melissa teaches others how to connect with their own intuitive nature and how to work with frequency for spiritual growth. She has appeared on number radio shows as both a guest and host. Melissa is the author of *365 Ways to Raise Your Frequency, Your Psychic Self, Animal Frequency, Earth Frequency, Llewellyn's Little Book of Spirit Animals, The Spirituality of Coziness, Simply Give Thanks* and many other titles. Her books with Llewellyn have been translated into multiple languages worldwide including Romanian, Russian, Chinese, French, Czech and Spanish. Please visit her website for a full list of her current titles.

Find Melissa Online at:
https://MelissaA.com
https://www.facebook.com/melissaalvarezauthor (main profile)
https://www.facebook.com/IamMelissaAlvarez (author page)

Other websites:
https://BookCovers.us
https://ThornRidge.com Online retail store
http://TopHatFriesians.com Barock Pinto & Friesian horses

The *365 Anonymous Quotes Journal* is a companion to my book, *365 Anonymous Quotes: Your Daily Dose of Encouraging and Entertaining Thoughts Throughout the Year*. Use the quotes as a writing prompt or as a guide when writing about your day.

Success is the proper utilization of failure.
Anonymous

Date: ________________

My thoughts for today: ____________________________________

You can only go as far as you push.
Anonymous

Date: ________________

My thoughts for today: ____________________________________

No one needs a smile as much as a person who fails to give one.

Anonymous

Date: ________________

My thoughts for today: ____________________________________

Happiness is a choice that requires effort at times.

Anonymous

Date: ________________

My thoughts for today: ____________________________________

When you reach for the stars, you may not get one, but you won't come up with a handful of mud, either.

Anonymous

Date: ________________

My thoughts for today: ______________________________

Failure is only the opportunity to begin again, this time more wisely.

Anonymous

Date: ________________

My thoughts for today: ____

Whatever you do, do well, and may success attend your efforts.

Anonymous

Date: ________________

My thoughts for today: ________________________________

Excuses are the tools with which persons with no purpose in view build for themselves, great monuments of nothing.

Anonymous

Date: ________________

My thoughts for today: ____________________________________

Forget mistakes. Organize victory out of mistakes.

Anonymous

Date: ________________

My thoughts for today: ____________________________________

Give yourself a compliment today and really listen.
Anonymous

Date: ________________

My thoughts for today: ____________________________________

Everywhere you go there are angels in disguise.
Anonymous

Date: ________________

My thoughts for today: ____________________________________

For problems, sweat is a good solvent.

Anonymous

Date: ________________

My thoughts for today: ________________

Happiness involves working towards meaningful goals.
Anonymous

Date: ______________

My thoughts for today: ______________

High expectations are the key to everything.

Anonymous

Date: ________________

My thoughts for today: ________________________________

If you don't know where you're going, you'll end up somewhere else.

Anonymous

Date: ________________

My thoughts for today: ________________________________

Improvement begins with "I".

Anonymous

Date: ________________

My thoughts for today: ________________________________

Knock the T off can't. You can if you think you can.

Anonymous

Date: ________________

My thoughts for today: ____________________________________

Make an effort everyday to feel good about who you are and what you can be.

Anonymous

Date: ________________

My thoughts for today: ________________

Never let a day go by without a dream.
Anonymous

Date: ________________

My thoughts for today: ____________________________________

Remember when you were at your best? Now be there again.
Anonymous

Date: ________________

My thoughts for today: ______________________________

The secret of action is to begin.

Anonymous

Date: ________________

My thoughts for today: ______________________________

There's no elevator to success. You have to take the stairs.

Anonymous

Date: ________________

My thoughts for today: ______________________________

Use it or lose it.

Anonymous

Date: ________________

My thoughts for today: ____________________________________

When things go wrong, don't go with them.

Anonymous

Date: ________________

My thoughts for today: ____________________________________

Exercise, you don't have time not to.

Anonymous

Date: ________________

My thoughts for today: ____________________________________

Ideas don't work unless you do.

Anonymous

Date: ________________

My thoughts for today: ________________________________

If you only look at what is, you might never attain what could be.

Anonymous

Date: ________________

My thoughts for today: ____________________________________

Think highly of yourself, for the world takes you at your own estimate.

Anonymous

Date: ________________

My thoughts for today: ________________

Sincerity gives wings to power.
Anonymous

Date: ________________

My thoughts for today: ____________________________________

If the truth be known, most successes are built on a multitude of failures.

Anonymous

Date: ________________

My thoughts for today: ____________________________________

Make your own destiny, don't wait for it to come to you, life is not a rehearsal!

Anonymous

Date: ________________

My thoughts for today: ________________________________

If you think positive, you can move a mountain in no time.

Anonymous

Date: ________________

My thoughts for today: ________________

Laughing helps. It's like jogging inside.

Anonymous

Date: ________________

My thoughts for today: ____________________________________

Anonymous kindness is powerful magic.
Anonymous

Date: ________________

My thoughts for today: ______________________________________

Don't get lost in the fabric of your personal drama.

Anonymous

Date: ________________

My thoughts for today: ____________________________________

Humor prevents hardening of the attitudes.
Anonymous

Date: ________________

My thoughts for today: ________________

The Pessimist curses the wind... The Optimist hopes it will change... The Realist adjusts the sails.

Anonymous

Date: ________________

My thoughts for today: ________________________________

I've learned - that we are responsible for what we do, no matter how we feel.

Anonymous

Date: ________________

My thoughts for today: ____________________________________

If you want to go to the fruit of the tree...You have to go out on a limb.

Anonymous

Date: ________________

My thoughts for today: ____________________________________

Obstacles are those frightful things you see when you take your eyes off your goals.

Anonymous

Date: ________________

My thoughts for today: ____________________________________

The difference between ordinary and extraordinary is that little extra.

Anonymous

Date: ________________

My thoughts for today: ____________________________________

Destiny is not a matter of chance, it is a matter of choice.

Anonymous

Date: ________________

My thoughts for today: ________________

Of all the things you wear, your expression is the most important.

Anonymous

Date: ________________

My thoughts for today: ____________________________________

Learn from the mistakes of others. You can't live long enough to make them all yourself.

Anonymous

Date: ________________

My thoughts for today: ____________________________________

Trust is the most valuable thing you will ever earn.

Anonymous

Date: ________________

My thoughts for today: ____________________________________

Each day comes bearing its gifts. Untie the ribbons.

Anonymous

Date: ________________

My thoughts for today: ________________________________

Laughter is the shock absorber that eases the blows of life.

Anonymous

Date: ________________

My thoughts for today: ____________________________________

There is nothing about a caterpillar that tells you it's going to be a butterfly.

Anonymous

Date: ________________

My thoughts for today: ________________________________

Your ego can be an asset or a liability depending on how you relate to it.

Anonymous

Date: ________________

My thoughts for today: ____________________________________

You will never get to where you want to be on dead hopes or hopeful wishing.

Anonymous

Date: ________________

My thoughts for today: ____________________________________

Today is the yesterday you worried about tomorrow.

Anonymous

Date: ________________

My thoughts for today: ____________________________________

You can only live once, but if you do it right, once is enough.

Anonymous

Date: ________________

My thoughts for today: ________________________________

Drifting through life without aim or purpose is the first cause of failure.

Anonymous

Date: ________________

My thoughts for today: ____________________________________

There is no failure. Only feedback.

Anonymous

Date: ________________

My thoughts for today: ____________________________________

Luck is when opportunity knocks and you answer.

Anonymous

Date: ________________

My thoughts for today: ____________________________________

Happiness is like jam. You can't spread a little without getting some on yourself.

Anonymous

Date: ________________

My thoughts for today: ____________________________________

Seeing yourself as you want to be is the key to personal growth.

Anonymous

Date: ________________

My thoughts for today: ____________________________________

We teach what we live.

Anonymous

Date: ________________

My thoughts for today: ____________________________________

The meaning of life is to give life meaning.
Anonymous

Date: __________________

My thoughts for today: ____________________________________

Faith is evidence of things unseen.

Anonymous

Date: ________________

My thoughts for today: ________________________________

If you can imagine it, you can achieve it, if you can dream it, you can become it.

Anonymous

Date: ________________

My thoughts for today: ____________________________________

The love we give away is the only love we keep.
Anonymous

Date: ________________

My thoughts for today: ____________________________________

He who knows others is wise. He who knows himself is enlightened.

Anonymous

Date: ________________

My thoughts for today: ____________________________________

The best way to predict your future is to create it.

Anonymous

Date: ________________

My thoughts for today: ____________________________________

You never really lose, until you quit trying.
Anonymous

Date: ________________

My thoughts for today: ____________________________________

We should not let success go to our heads, or our failures go to our hearts.

Anonymous

Date: ________________

My thoughts for today: ________________________________

A friend is one who believes in you when you have ceased to believe in yourself.

Anonymous

Date: ________________

My thoughts for today: ________________________________

The only thing in life achieved without effort is failure.

Anonymous

Date: ________________

My thoughts for today: ____________________________________

Anyone who says sunshine brings happiness has never danced in the rain.

Anonymous

Date: ________________

My thoughts for today: ____________________________________

It's not who you are that holds you back, it's who you think you're not.

Anonymous

Date: ________________

My thoughts for today: ________________________________

Dreams and dedication are a powerful combination.

Anonymous

Date: ________________

My thoughts for today: ________________________________

Finding fault is easy. It's improving that's hard.

Anonymous

Date: ________________

My thoughts for today: ______________________________

Joy can find you wherever you are.
Anonymous

Date: ________________

My thoughts for today: ____________________________________

You are a blessing that someone else counts.

Anonymous

Date: ________________

My thoughts for today: ___________________________________

Think of today as a beautiful place you've never been.

Anonymous

Date: ________________

My thoughts for today: ____________________________________

The poorest man is not without a cent but without a dream.

Anonymous

Date: ________________

My thoughts for today: ____________________________________

Great visions often start with small dreams.

Anonymous

Date: ________________

My thoughts for today: ____________________________________

Habit is like a soft bed, easy to get into but hard to get out of.

Anonymous

Date: ________________

My thoughts for today: ____________________________________

Let each day be your masterpiece.
Anonymous

Date: ________________

My thoughts for today: ____________________________________

Forget mistakes. Organize victory out of mistakes.

Anonymous

Date: ________________

My thoughts for today: ____________________________________

If you wait, all that happens is that you get older.

Anonymous

Date: ________________

My thoughts for today: ____________________________________

Nothing is hard if you try.

Anonymous

Date: ________________

My thoughts for today: ________________________________

Passion is the trigger of success.

Anonymous

Date: ______________

My thoughts for today: ______________________________

The more clear you are on what you want, the more power you will have.

Anonymous

Date: ________________

My thoughts for today: ____________________________________

If it is to be, it is up to me.

Anonymous

Date: ________________

My thoughts for today: ____________________________________

Losers let it happen. Winners make it happen.

Anonymous

Date: ________________

My thoughts for today: ____________________________________

Morale is when your hand and feet keep on working when your head simply says it can't be done.

Anonymous

Date: ________________

My thoughts for today: ____________________________________

The best angle from which to approach any problem is the try-angle.

Anonymous

Date: ________________

My thoughts for today: ____________________________________

The task ahead of us is never as great as the power behind us.

Anonymous

Date: ________________

My thoughts for today: ____________________________________

Most people are in favor of progress, it's the changes they don't like.

Anonymous

Date: ________________

My thoughts for today: ____________________________________

Know yourself, master yourself, conquest of self is most gratifying.

Anonymous

Date: ________________

My thoughts for today: ____________________________________

Take pride in how far you have come, have faith in how far you can go.

Anonymous

Date: ________________

My thoughts for today: ______________________________

Years wrinkle the skin, but lack of enthusiasm wrinkles the soul.

Anonymous

Date: ________________

My thoughts for today: ________________________________

Never let yesterday's disappointments overshadow tomorrow's dreams.

Anonymous

Date: ________________

My thoughts for today: ____________________________________

Form good habits. They are just as hard to break as the bad ones!

Anonymous

Date: ________________

My thoughts for today: ____

The only consistency in life is change.
Anonymous

Date: ________________

My thoughts for today: ________________________________

If I want circumstances in my life to change for the better, I must change for the better.

Anonymous

Date: ________________

My thoughts for today: ____________________________________

Ideas are funny little things. They won't work unless you do.

Anonymous

Date: ________________

My thoughts for today: ________________________________

Choose your actions carefully. What you do right now is creating the future in your world.

Anonymous

Date: ________________

My thoughts for today: ____________________________________

A deadline has a marvelous ability to concentrate the mind.

Anonymous

Date: ________________

My thoughts for today: ____

Triumph --umph added to try.

Anonymous

Date: ________________

My thoughts for today: ____

All life is connected. When one part is damaged everything else is affected.

Anonymous

Date: ________________

My thoughts for today: ________________

If you don't hear opportunity knocking, find another door.
Anonymous

Date: ________________

My thoughts for today: ______________________________

Keep your head and your heart going in the right direction and you will not have to worry about your feet.

Anonymous

Date: ________________

My thoughts for today: ____________________________________

Ignorance, or refusal to believe.

Anonymous

Date: ________________

My thoughts for today: ________________________________

When the going seems easy, you may be going downhill.

Anonymous

Date: ________________

My thoughts for today: ________________________________

Footprints on the sands of time are never made by sitting down.

Anonymous

Date: ________________

My thoughts for today: ______________________________

Do not follow where the path may lead, go instead where there is no path and leave a trail.

Anonymous

Date: ________________

My thoughts for today: ____________________________________

When Better is possible, then Good is not enough.

Anonymous

Date: ________________

My thoughts for today: ____________________________________

To be a star, you must shine your own light, follow your own path, and don't worry about the darkness, for that is when the stars shine brightest.

Anonymous

Date: ________________

My thoughts for today: ________________________________

If nothing ever changed, there'd be no butterflies.

Anonymous

Date: ________________

My thoughts for today: ___________________________________

A smile is the light in the window of the soul indicating that the heart is home.

Anonymous

Date: ________________

My thoughts for today: ____________________________________

Don't ever save anything for a special occasion. Being alive is a special occasion.

Anonymous

Date: ________________

My thoughts for today: ____________________________________

If you don't have time to do it right, you must have time to do it over.

Anonymous

Date: ________________

My thoughts for today: ____________________________________

Purpose serves as a principal around which to organize our lives.

Anonymous

Date: ________________

My thoughts for today: ____________________________________

When you delight in the game the effort seems unimportant.
Anonymous

Date: ________________

My thoughts for today: ________________________________

Life is a cup to be filled, not drained.

Anonymous

Date: ________________

My thoughts for today: ____________________________________

A smile costs you nothing. It's a little thing, but will always produce big results.

Anonymous

Date: ________________

My thoughts for today: ____________________________________

Life is beautiful when you burn every second doing something that matters.

Anonymous

Date: ________________

My thoughts for today: ____________________________________

Minds are like parachutes...They only function when open.
Anonymous

Date: ________________

My thoughts for today: ____________________________________

Behold the turtle; he only goes forward when his neck is stuck out.

Anonymous

Date: ________________

My thoughts for today: ______________________________

You can make good choices, you can make rotten choices, but you can make choices.

Anonymous

Date: ________________

My thoughts for today: ____________________________________

Yin and Yang: A blend of opposites for perfect harmony.

Anonymous

Date: ________________

My thoughts for today: ____________________________________

We can do anything we want if we stick to it long enough.

Anonymous

Date: ________________

My thoughts for today: ________________________________

Failure is the path of least persistence.

Anonymous

Date: ________________

My thoughts for today: ____________________________________

The key to everything is patience! You get the chicken by hatching the egg, not by smashing it.

Anonymous

Date: ________________

My thoughts for today: ____________________________________

Excellence is best described as doing the right things right - selecting the most important things and then accomplishing them 100% correctly.

Anonymous

Date: ________________

My thoughts for today: ____________________________________

Every accomplishment starts with the decision to try.

Anonymous

Date: ______________

My thoughts for today: ______________________________

Winners know that accomplishment is the result of activity.

Anonymous

Date: ________________

My thoughts for today: ____________________________________

It doesn't matter what you can do, what matters is what you will do.

Anonymous

Date: ________________

My thoughts for today: ________________

Challenges can be stepping stones or stumbling blocks. It's just a matter of how you view them.

Anonymous

Date: ________________

My thoughts for today: ____________________________________

Your vision will become clear only when you look into your heart, those who look outside Dream, those who look inside Awaken.

Anonymous

Date: ________________

My thoughts for today: ________________________________

It's not the obstacle we conquer, but ourselves.
Anonymous

Date: ________________

My thoughts for today: ____________________________________

There will never be another now, so I will make the most of today. There will never be another me, so I will make the most of myself.

Anonymous

Date: ________________

My thoughts for today: ____________________________________

Don't just exist, Live.

Anonymous

Date: ________________

My thoughts for today: ____________________________________

Champions believe in themselves even if no one else does.

Anonymous

Date: ________________

My thoughts for today: ____________________________________

Impossibility is an opinion, not a fact.
Anonymous

Date: ________________

My thoughts for today: ____________________________________

Procrastination is the natural assassin of opportunity.
Anonymous

Date: ________________

My thoughts for today: ______________________________

Keep your face always toward the sunshine, and the shadows will fall behind you.

Anonymous

Date: ________________

My thoughts for today: ____________________________________

You've only failed, If you've failed to try.

Anonymous

Date: ________________

My thoughts for today: ________________________________

All we are given is possibilities to make of ourselves one thing or another.

Anonymous

Date: ________________

My thoughts for today: ____________________________________

It can't be done are being passed by those doing it.

Anonymous

Date: ________________

My thoughts for today: ______________________________

A smile is contagious – start an epidemic!
Anonymous

Date: ________________

My thoughts for today: ____

No one can choose your mountain or tell you when to climb
It's yours alone to challenge at your own pace and time.

Anonymous

Date: ________________

My thoughts for today: ______________________________

The future belongs to those who see possibilities before they become obvious.

Anonymous

Date: ________________

My thoughts for today: ____________________________________

Reach high, for stars lie hidden in your soul. Dream deep, for every dream precedes the goal.

Anonymous

Date: ________________

My thoughts for today: ________________________________

Success is getting what you want, Happiness is liking what you get.

Anonymous

Date: ________________

My thoughts for today: ____________________________________

There are no shortcuts to any place worth going.

Anonymous

Date: ________________

My thoughts for today: ________________________________

If your life is free of failures, you're not taking enough risks.
Anonymous

Date: ________________

My thoughts for today: ____________________________________

Obstacles are put in our way to see if we really want something or we just thought we did.

Anonymous

Date: ________________

My thoughts for today: ______________________________________

The road to success is not doing one thing 100 percent better, but doing 100 things one percent better.

Anonymous

Date: ________________

My thoughts for today: ____________________________________

If you want to get a pail of milk, don't sit yourself on a stool in the middle of a field hoping that a cow will come over to you.

Anonymous

Date: ________________

My thoughts for today: ________________________________

If you find a path with no obstacles--it is probably a path that doesn't lead anywhere.

Anonymous

Date: ______________

My thoughts for today: ______________________________

Set your mind on a definite goal and observe how quickly the world stands aside to let you pass.

Anonymous

Date: ________________

My thoughts for today: ________________________________

Inspiration comes from watching others, Motivation comes from within.

Anonymous

Date: ________________

My thoughts for today: ____________________________________

The only person you need to prove anything to is yourself.

Anonymous

Date: ________________

My thoughts for today: ____________________________________

**If you have discipline, you can conquer the world.
If you don't have discipline, the world will conquer you.**

Anonymous

Date: ________________

My thoughts for today: ____________________________________

Follow your heart and you'll never get lost.

Anonymous

Date: ________________

My thoughts for today: ________________________________

Some dream of doing great things, while others stay awake and get on with it.

Anonymous

Date: ________________

My thoughts for today: ____________________________________

Whoever is happy will make others happy too.

Anonymous

Date: ________________

My thoughts for today: ____________________________________

The positive thinker sees the invisible, feels the intangible, and achieves the impossible.

Anonymous

Date: ________________

My thoughts for today: ____________________________________

If you expect nothing but the best you might get it.

Anonymous

Date: ________________

My thoughts for today: ____________________________________

The greatest pleasure in life is doing what people say you cannot.

Anonymous

Date: ________________

My thoughts for today: ____________________________________

Time invested in improving ourselves cuts down on time wasted in disapproving of others.

Anonymous

Date: ________________

My thoughts for today: ________________________________

What comes around goes around.

Anonymous

Date: ________________

My thoughts for today: ____________________________________

What you achieve through the journey of life is not as important as who you become.

Anonymous

Date: ________________

My thoughts for today: ____________________________________

Think big, believe big, act big, and the results will be big.

Anonymous

Date: ________________

My thoughts for today: ____________________________________

The difference between a pipe dream and a great idea is persistence.

Anonymous

Date: ________________

My thoughts for today: ____________________________________

All easy problems have already been solved.

Anonymous

Date: ________________

My thoughts for today: ____________________________________

Do not follow where the path may lead....go instead where there is no path and leave a trail.

Anonymous

Date: ________________

My thoughts for today: ________________________________

When your dreams turn to dust; vacuum.

Anonymous

Date: ________________

My thoughts for today: ____________________________________

Find expression for a sorrow and it will become dear to you. Find expression for a joy, and you will intensify its ecstasy.

Anonymous

Date: ________________

My thoughts for today: ________________

Good judgment comes from experience, and experience--well, that comes from poor judgment.

Anonymous

Date: ________________

My thoughts for today: ____________________________________

Include the success of others in your dreams for your own success.

Anonymous

Date: ________________

My thoughts for today: ________________________________

Keep your head and your heart going in the right direction and you will not have to worry about your feet.

Anonymous

Date: ________________

My thoughts for today: ____________________________________

Minds are like parachutes - they only function when open.

Anonymous

Date: ________________

My thoughts for today: ____________________________________

Nobody trips over mountains. It is the small pebble that causes you to stumble. Pass all the pebbles in your path and you will find you have crossed the mountain.

Anonymous

Date: ______________

My thoughts for today: ______________________________

One essential to success is that you desire be an all-obsessing one, your thoughts and aims be coordinated, and your energy be concentrated and applied without letup.

Anonymous

Date: ________________

My thoughts for today: ____

The one who says it cannot be done should never interrupt the one who is doing it.

Anonymous

Date: ________________

My thoughts for today: ____________________________________

To be a winner, all you need to give is all you have.

Anonymous

Date: ________________

My thoughts for today: ____________________________________

Today is the yesterday you worried about tomorrow.

Anonymous

Date: ________________

My thoughts for today: ____________________________________

When the tide of life turns against you, And the current upsets your boat, Don't waste tears on what might have been Just lie on your back and float.

Anonymous

Date: ________________

My thoughts for today: ____________________________________

All of us could take a lesson from the weather. It pays no attention to criticism.

Anonymous

Date: ________________

My thoughts for today: ____________________________________

Learn from yesterday, live for today, hope for tomorrow.

Anonymous

Date: ________________

My thoughts for today: ____________________________________

Bite off more than you can chew, then chew it. Plan more than you can do, then do it.

Anonymous

Date: ________________

My thoughts for today: ____________________________________

Everything is susceptible to change, don't fear it, embrace it, after all you can't go back but there's always a new chapter of life just waiting to be written.

Anonymous

Date: ________________

My thoughts for today: ____________________________________

Contentment is not the fulfillment of what you want, but the realization of how much you already have.

Anonymous

Date: ________________

My thoughts for today: ____________________________________

Don't let yourself forget what it's like to be sixteen.

Anonymous

Date: ________________

My thoughts for today: ____________________________________

Happiness is a choice that requires effort at times.

Anonymous

Date: ________________

My thoughts for today: ____________________________________

It is wise to keep in mind that no success or failure is necessarily final.

Anonymous

Date: ________________

My thoughts for today: ____________________________________

Some people weave burlap into the fabric of our lives, and some weave gold thread. Both contribute to make the whole picture beautiful and unique.

Anonymous

Date: ________________

My thoughts for today: ____________________________________

Success is not the key to happiness. Happiness is the key to success. If you love what you are doing, you will be successful.

Anonymous

Date: ________________

My thoughts for today: ____________________________________

The positive thinker sees the invisible, feels the intangible, and achieves the impossible.

Anonymous

Date: ______________

My thoughts for today: ______________________________

The real measure of your wealth is how much you'd be worth if you lost all your money.

Anonymous

Date: ________________

My thoughts for today: ____________________________________

The smallest good deed is better than the grandest intention.

Anonymous

Date: ________________

My thoughts for today: ____________________________________

What people respect is one thing, what people envy is the other. What people respect they do not always want to do, be or have. If, then, you want to be respected, and respect yourself, you sometimes need to do more than you want to.

Anonymous

Date: ________________

My thoughts for today: ______________________________

Whatever you undertake, act with prudence, and consider the consequences.

Anonymous

Date: ________________

My thoughts for today: ____________________________________

The highest happiness of man is to have probed what is knowable and quietly to revere what is unknowable.

Anonymous

Date: ________________

My thoughts for today: ____________________________________

If you want to achieve greatness stop asking for permission.

Anonymous

Date: ______________

My thoughts for today: ______________________________

To live a creative life, we must lose our fear of being wrong.

Anonymous

Date: ________________

My thoughts for today: ____________________________________

Trust because you are willing to accept the risk, not because it's safe or certain.

Anonymous

Date: ________________

My thoughts for today: ____________________________________

Good things come to people who wait, but better things come to those who go out and get them.

Anonymous

Date: ________________

My thoughts for today: ________________________________

If you do what you always did, you will get what you always got.

Anonymous

Date: ________________

My thoughts for today: ____________________________________

Successful entrepreneurs are givers and not takers of positive energy.

Anonymous

Date: ________________

My thoughts for today: ____________________________________

The ones who are crazy enough to think they can change the world, are the ones that do.

Anonymous

Date: ________________

My thoughts for today: ____________________________________

Don't raise your voice, improve your argument.

Anonymous

Date: ________________

My thoughts for today: ____________________________________

The meaning of life is to find your gift. The purpose of life is to give it away.

Anonymous

Date: ________________

My thoughts for today: ____________________________________

Blessed are those who can give without remembering and take without forgetting.

Anonymous

Date: ________________

My thoughts for today: ____________________________________

Do one thing every day that scares you.

Anonymous

Date: ________________

My thoughts for today: ________________________________

What's the point of being alive if you don't at least try to do something remarkable.

Anonymous

Date: ________________

My thoughts for today: ____________________________________

Knowledge is being aware of what you can do. Wisdom is knowing when not to do it.

Anonymous

Date: ________________

My thoughts for today: ________________________________

Your problem isn't the problem. Your reaction is the problem.

Anonymous

Date: ________________

My thoughts for today: ______________________________________

You can do anything, but not everything.

Anonymous

Date: ________________

My thoughts for today: ____________________________________

It's not what you look at that matters, it's what you see.

Anonymous

Date: ________________

My thoughts for today: ________________________________

Sometimes we are limited more by attitude than by opportunities.

Anonymous

Date: ________________

My thoughts for today: ____________________________________

A healthy attitude is contagious but don't wait to catch it from others. Be a carrier.

Anonymous

Date: ________________

My thoughts for today: ____

Although fate presents the circumstances, how you react depends on your character.

Anonymous

Date: ________________

My thoughts for today: ________________________________

Attitude determines altitude.

Anonymous

Date: ________________

My thoughts for today: ________________________________

Take charge of your attitude. Don't let someone else choose it for you.

Anonymous

Date: ________________

My thoughts for today: ____________________________________

Attitudes are contagious. Are yours worth catching?

Anonymous

Date: ________________

My thoughts for today: ________________________________

People who say it cannot be done should not interrupt those who are doing it.

Anonymous

Date: ________________

My thoughts for today: ____________________________________

When you were born, you were crying and everyone around you was smiling. Live your life so that when you die, you're smiling and everyone around you is crying.

Anonymous

Date: ________________

My thoughts for today: ____________________________________

Unwavering obedience to the true principals we learn will assure us spiritual survival.

Anonymous

Date: ________________

My thoughts for today: ____________________________________

Happiness will never come to those who fail to appreciate what they already have.

Anonymous

Date: ________________

My thoughts for today: ____________________________________

To the world you are just one person, but to one person you could mean the world.

Anonymous

Date: ________________

My thoughts for today: ________________________________

Happiness is like a butterfly. The more you chase it, the more it eludes you. But if you turn your attention to other things, It comes and sits softly on your shoulder.

Anonymous

Date: ________________

My thoughts for today: ____________________________________

How a man plays a game shows something of his character, how he loses shows all of it.

Anonymous

Date: ________________

My thoughts for today: ____________________________________

You haven't failed until you quite trying.
Anonymous

Date: ________________

My thoughts for today: ______________________________

Success is the proper utilization of failure.

Anonymous

Date: ________________

My thoughts for today: ____________________________________

You're on the road to success when you realize that failure is only a detour.

Anonymous

Date: ________________

My thoughts for today: ____________________________________

We more frequently fail to face the right problem than fail to solve the problem we face.

Anonymous

Date: ________________

My thoughts for today: ____________________________________

How a man plays a game shows something of his character, how he loses shows all of it.

Anonymous

Date: ________________

My thoughts for today: ________________________________

Pep without purpose is piffle.

Anonymous

Date: ________________

My thoughts for today: ____________________________________

You can't expect people to look eye to eye with you if you are looking down on them.

Anonymous

Date: ________________

My thoughts for today: ____________________________________

You can tell more about a person by what he says about others than you can by what others say about him.

Anonymous

Date: ________________

My thoughts for today: ________________________________

A man never likes you so well as when he leaves your company liking himself.

Anonymous

Date: ________________

My thoughts for today: ____________________________________

People don't care how much you know, until they know how much you care.

Anonymous

Date: ________________

My thoughts for today: ________________________________

Love is blind, but friendship closes it's eyes.

Anonymous

Date: ________________

My thoughts for today: ____________________________________

A smooth sea never made a skillful mariner.

Anonymous

Date: ________________

My thoughts for today: ______________________________________

Attitude determines altitude.
Anonymous

Date: ________________

My thoughts for today: ________________________________

Only those who do nothing at all make no mistakes…but that would be a mistake.

Anonymous

Date: ______________

My thoughts for today: ______________________________

He who dares nothing need hope for nothing.

Anonymous

Date: ______________

My thoughts for today: ______________________________

It is quite possible to work without results, but never will there be results without work.

Anonymous

Date: ________________

My thoughts for today: ____________________________________

The daily grind of hard work gets a person polished.
Anonymous

Date: ________________

My thoughts for today: ____________________________________

When you reach for the stars, you may not get one, but you won't come up with a handful of mud, either.

Anonymous

Date: ________________

My thoughts for today: ____________________________________

There is no chance, no fate, no destiny that can circumvent, or hinder, or control a firm resolve of a determined soul.

Anonymous

Date: ________________

My thoughts for today: ____________________________________

The successful man is the average man, focused.
Anonymous

Date: ________________

My thoughts for today: ___________________________________

If you are willing to do more than you are paid to do, eventually you will be paid to do more than you do.

Anonymous

Date: ________________

My thoughts for today: ____________________________________

I will not should on myself today.

Anonymous

Date: ________________

My thoughts for today: ____________________________________

Nothing changes until you do.
Anonymous

Date: ________________

My thoughts for today: ____________________________________

Listen a hundred times. Ponder a thousand times. Speak once.

Anonymous

Date: ________________

My thoughts for today: ___________________________________

Re-shape yourself thru the power of your will.
Anonymous

Date: ________________

My thoughts for today: ____________________________________

If you want something done, give it to a busy man.

Anonymous

Date: ________________

My thoughts for today: ____________________________________

The person who doesn't read is no better off than the person who can't read.

Anonymous

Date: ________________

My thoughts for today: ____________________________________

Always act as if success was guaranteed.
Anonymous

Date: ________________

My thoughts for today: ____________________________________

Those who take bold chances don't think failure is the opposite of success. They believe complacency is.

Anonymous

Date: ________________

My thoughts for today: ________________________________

Risk takers: their goal in life is not to succeed, make money, be happy or be anything other than engaged.

Anonymous

Date: ________________

My thoughts for today: ____________________________________

It is not a disgrace to fail...one must analyze each failure and find its cause...he must learn how to fail intelligently. Failing is one of the greatest arts in the world. One fails toward success.

Anonymous

Date: ________________

My thoughts for today: ____________________________________

Rather than cripple, failure can strengthen. Depending on how we respond to them, blows can shatter us as if we were a cheap clay pot or temper us as they would steel.

Anonymous

Date: ________________

My thoughts for today: ____________________________________

If you haven't failed, you're not trying hard enough.
Anonymous

Date: ________________

My thoughts for today: ____________________________________

Not only is there little stigma attributed to going bankrupt among cutting-edge entrepreneurs, it's even seen as a good source of business experience.

Anonymous

Date: ________________

My thoughts for today: ____________________________________

Failure's pain subsides faster than the ache of regret.

Anonymous

Date: ________________

My thoughts for today: ________________________________

In the long run, avoiding activity that might hurt causes more agony than acting, failing, and dealing with the pain.

Anonymous

Date: ________________

My thoughts for today: ________________________________

Too many of those with unrealized aspirations have set them aside due to fear of failure. The bigger the dream, the greater the fear. Doing less than our best allays this fear. I could have done better if I'd tried, we assure ourselves. Among the least appreciated reasons for doing superficial, second-rate work of any kind is the comfort of knowing it's not our best that's on the line. By not trying too hard, we avoid learning what our true potential is, and having to fulfill it. Doing our best can be deeply threatening. It forces us to consider what we're actually capable of accomplishing. Once we learn that lesson, we can't unlearn it. Our true potential becomes both a shining light we can follow and an oppressive burden of expectation that might, or might not, be met.

Anonymous

Date: ________________

My thoughts for today: ____________________________________

The world belongs to those who don't let anxiety about screwing up keep them from moving forward.

Anonymous

Date: ________________

My thoughts for today: ____________________________________

Those who are too afraid to make a mistake work for those who aren't.

Anonymous

Date: ________________

My thoughts for today: ____________________________________

If I have an art form of leadership, it is to make as many mistakes as quickly as I can in order to learn.

Anonymous

Date: ________________

My thoughts for today: ___________________________________

"A man's life is interesting primarily when he has failed—I well know," said the French statesman, Georges Clemenceau, "for it's a sign that he tried to surpass himself."

Anonymous

Date: ________________

My thoughts for today: ________________________________

To the true innovator, there's no such thing as a mistake. Each miscue is considered part of the process, a marker on the map that says where not to go.

Anonymous

Date: ________________

My thoughts for today: ________________________________

Imperfections are the essence of evolution.

Anonymous

Date: ________________

My thoughts for today: ____________________________________

Creative minds have already embraced the symbolic nature of success and failure...failure, they say, is a "step on the road to success..."

Anonymous

Date: ________________

My thoughts for today: ____________________________________

Some consider setbacks a badge of honor, unmistakable proof they're bold risk takers. Far from hiding their blunders, they brag about them.

Anonymous

Date: ________________

My thoughts for today: ________________

Pursuing success is like chasing the horizon, and failure is an integral part of an interesting life.

Anonymous

Date: ________________

My thoughts for today: ____________________________________

Thinking well is wise; planning well, wiser; but doing well is the wisest and best of all.

Anonymous

Date: ________________

My thoughts for today: ____________________________________

Perfect love is to feeling what perfect white is to color. Many think that white is the absence of color. It is not. It is the inclusion of all color. White is every other color that exists combined. So, too, is love not the absence of emotion (hatred, anger, lust, jealousy, covertness), but the summation of all feeling? It is the sum total. The aggregate amount. The everything.

Anonymous

Date: ________________

My thoughts for today: ____________________________________

It's a sin to be poor!" He wasn't referring to moral turpitude, but rather to "the frustration of potentiality." He believed and taught that, when we establish ourselves in the consciousness of God, the whole universe moves to flow into us with its abundance of life and substance. This is obviously what Jesus had in mind when he said, "But seek first his kingdom and his righteousness, and all these things shall be yours as well.

Anonymous

Date: ________________

My thoughts for today: ________________________________

The key to keeping your balance is knowing when you've lost it.

Anonymous

Date: ________________

My thoughts for today: ________________________________

The human heart knows when it is being asked to be less.

Anonymous

Date: ________________

My thoughts for today: ____________________________________

Whatever we feel we most need is what we most need to give.

Anonymous

Date: ________________

My thoughts for today: ____________________________________

A habit is only a habit until you can observe it. And then it's a choice.

Anonymous

Date: ________________

My thoughts for today: ____________________________________

The chief cause of suffering for human beings is an inability to have things be the way they are.

Anonymous

Date: ________________

My thoughts for today: ____________________________________

The only job where you start at the top, is digging a hole.

Anonymous

Date: ________________

My thoughts for today: ____________________________________

Once the game is over, the king and the pawn go back in the same box.

Anonymous

Date: ________________

My thoughts for today: ____________________________________

The best place to find a helping hand is at the end of your own arm.

Anonymous

Date: ________________

My thoughts for today: ________________________________

Your current safe boundaries were once unknown frontiers.

Anonymous

Date: ________________

My thoughts for today: ________________________________

Seldom does and individual exceed his own expectations.

Anonymous

Date: ________________

My thoughts for today: ________________________________

Your talent is God's gift to you. What you do with it is your gift back to God.

Anonymous

Date: ________________

My thoughts for today: ____________________________________

Anyone who thinks the sky is the limit, has limited imagination.

Anonymous

Date: ________________

My thoughts for today: ____________________________________

Minds are like parachutes, they function only when open.

Anonymous

Date: ________________

My thoughts for today: ________________________________

Some minds are like concrete, all mixed up and permanently set.

Anonymous

Date: ________________

My thoughts for today: ____________________________________

There is only one rule to become a good talker, learn how to listen.

Anonymous

Date: ________________

My thoughts for today: ____________________________________

Hardening of the heart ages people faster than hardening of the arteries.

Anonymous

Date: ________________

My thoughts for today: ________________________________

It's easier to prepare and prevent, that to repair and repent.

Anonymous

Date: ________________

My thoughts for today: ____________________________________

Sacrifice is giving up something good for something better.

Anonymous

Date: ________________

My thoughts for today: ____________________________________

A smile is a curve that sets everything straight.
Anonymous

Date: ______________

My thoughts for today: ______________________________

A smile is a light in the window of the soul indicating that the heart is at home.

Anonymous

Date: ________________

My thoughts for today: ________________________________

Smile: if you can't lift the corners, let the middle sag.

Anonymous

Date: ______________

My thoughts for today: ______________________________

A smile is an inexpensive way to improve your looks.

Anonymous

Date: ________________

My thoughts for today: ____________________________________

A strong person and a waterfall always channel their own path.

Anonymous

Date: ________________

My thoughts for today: ____________________________________

The difference between 'involvement' and 'commitment' is like an eggs and ham breakfast: the chicken was 'involved' - the pig was 'committed'.

Anonymous

Date: ________________

My thoughts for today: ____________________________________

So much of what we know of love we learn as home.
Anonymous

Date: ________________

My thoughts for today: ____________________________________

I'm not a failure if I don't make it... I'm a success because I tried.

Anonymous

Date: ________________

My thoughts for today: ________________

Achieving starts with believing.
Anonymous

Date: ________________

My thoughts for today: ____________________________________

Action speaks louder than words - but not nearly as often.

Anonymous

Date: ________________

My thoughts for today: ____________________________________

A person who aims at nothing is sure to hit it.

Anonymous

Date: ______________

My thoughts for today: ______________________________

A smile is a window on your face to show your heart is at home.

Anonymous

Date: ________________

My thoughts for today: ____________________________________

A word of encouragement during a failure is worth more than an hour of praise after success.

Anonymous

Date: ________________

My thoughts for today: ____________________________________

All the so-called "secrets of success" will not work unless you do.

Anonymous

Date: ________________

My thoughts for today: ____________________________________

Although at the moment they may be equal in their lack of a real answer, the man who replies I'll find out, is much more valuable to his employer, his neighbor, and to himself than the man who replies l don't know.

Anonymous

Date: ________________

My thoughts for today: ____________________________________

A healthy attitude is contagious but don't wait to catch it from others. Be a carrier.

Anonymous

Date: ________________

My thoughts for today: ____________________________________

A person shows what he is by what he does with what he has.
Anonymous

Date: ________________

My thoughts for today: ____________________________________

Although fate presents the circumstances, how you react depends on your character.

Anonymous

Date: ________________

My thoughts for today: ________________

An important project was begun, a bishop quoted an ancient sage as saying, "If our thoughts and hopes are elsewhere, it is impossible for us to set our faces steadily toward the work required of us."

Anonymous

Date: ______________

My thoughts for today: ________________________________

Failure is the path of least persistence.

Anonymous

Date: ________________

My thoughts for today: ____

Goals that are not written down are just wishes.

Anonymous

Date: ________________

My thoughts for today: ____________________________________

God does not ask about our ability, but our availability.

Anonymous

Date: ________________

My thoughts for today: ____________________________________

God gives us dreams a size too big so that we can grow in them.

Anonymous

Date: ________________

My thoughts for today: ____________________________________

His mother asked him why he said that when the day was anything but beautiful. Mother, said he, with rare wisdom, never judge a day by its weather.

Anonymous

Date: ________________

My thoughts for today: ____________________________________

I can alter my life by altering the attitude of my mind.

Anonymous

Date: ________________

My thoughts for today: ____________________________________

Ideas are funny little things. They don't work unless you do.

Anonymous

Date: ________________

My thoughts for today: ____________________________________

If you aim at nothing, you'll hit it every time.

Anonymous

Date: ________________

My thoughts for today: ____________________________________

If you chase two rabbits, both will escape.

Anonymous

Date: ________________

My thoughts for today: ________________________________

If you don't climb the mountain, you can't view the plain.

Anonymous

Date: ________________

My thoughts for today: ____________________________________

In order to succeed, you must first be willing to fail.
Anonymous

Date: ________________

My thoughts for today: ____________________________________

In the darkest hour the soul is replenished and given strength to continue and endure.

Anonymous

Date: ________________

My thoughts for today: ____________________________________

It is wise to keep in mind that no success or failure is necessarily final.

Anonymous

Date: ________________

My thoughts for today: ____

It's not the work that's hard, it's the discipline.

Anonymous

Date: ______________

My thoughts for today: ______________________________

Never be afraid to do something new. Remember, amateurs built the ark; professionals built the titanic.

Anonymous

Date: ________________

My thoughts for today: ___________________________________

No duty is more urgent than that of returning thanks.

Anonymous

Date: ________________

My thoughts for today: ____________________________________

One of the most difficult things to give away is kindness; it usually comes back to you.

Anonymous

Date: ________________

My thoughts for today: ____________________________________

Only those who do nothing make no mistakes.
Anonymous

Date: ________________

My thoughts for today: ____________________________________

Remember that great love and great achievements involve great risk.

Anonymous

Date: ________________

My thoughts for today: ____________________________________

Reputation is the shell a man discards when he leaves life for immortality. His character he takes with him.

Anonymous

Date: ________________

My thoughts for today: ____________________________________

Reputation is what the world thinks a man is; character is what he really is.

Anonymous

Date: ________________

My thoughts for today: ________________________________

Self-determination is fine but needs to be tempered with self-control.

Anonymous

Date: ________________

My thoughts for today: ____________________________________

Some people grin and bear it; others smile and do it.

Anonymous

Date: ________________

My thoughts for today: ________________________________

Sometimes we are limited more by attitude than by opportunities.

Anonymous

Date: ________________

My thoughts for today: ______________________________

Take charge of your attitude. Don't let someone else choose it for you.

Anonymous

Date: ________________

My thoughts for today: ____________________________________

The harder you fall, the higher you bounce.

Anonymous

Date: ______________

My thoughts for today: ______________

The only real failure in life is the failure to try.

Anonymous

Date: ________________

My thoughts for today: ________________________________

The true gentleman does not preach his beliefs until he does so by his actions.

Anonymous

Date: ________________

My thoughts for today: ____________________________________

When the world says, "Give up," hope whispers, "Try it one more time."

Anonymous

Date: ________________

My thoughts for today: ____________________________________

The best way to finish an unpleasant task is to get started.

Anonymous

Date: ________________

My thoughts for today: ____________________________________

Faith is like electricity. You can't see it, but you can see the light.

Anonymous

Date: ________________

My thoughts for today: ____________________________________

When your life flashes before your eyes, make sure you've got plenty to watch.

Anonymous

Date: ________________

My thoughts for today: ____________________________________

Some people dream of great accomplishments, while others stay awake and do them.

Anonymous

Date: ________________

My thoughts for today: ____________________________________

The first step toward creating an improved future is developing the ability to envision it.

Anonymous

Date: ________________

My thoughts for today: ____________________________________

Do not worry about whether or not the sun will rise. Be prepared to enjoy it

Anonymous

Date: ________________

My thoughts for today: ________________________________

Set aside half an hour every day to do all your worrying; then take a nap during this period.

Anonymous

Date: ________________

My thoughts for today: ________________

Worry: a sustained form of fear caused by indecision

Anonymous

Date: ________________

My thoughts for today: ____________________________________

God in His goodness sent the grapes, to cheer both great and small; little fools will drink too much, and great fools not at all.

Anonymous

Date: ________________

My thoughts for today: ____________________________________

Good judgment comes from experience; and experience, well, that comes from bad judgment.

Anonymous

Date: ________________

My thoughts for today: ________________________________

Laughter is a tranquilizer with no side effects.
Anonymous

Date: ________________

My thoughts for today: ________________

Experience is the hardest kind of teacher. It gives you the test first, and the lesson afterward.

Anonymous

Date: ________________

My thoughts for today: ____________________________________

The highest happiness of man is to have probed what is knowable and quietly to revere what is unknowable.

Anonymous

Date: ________________

My thoughts for today: ________________________________

When things go wrong, don't go with them.

Anonymous

Date: ________________

My thoughts for today: ____________________________________

It is better to remain silent and thought a fool, than to open your mouth and remove all doubt.

Anonymous

Date: ________________

My thoughts for today: ____________________________________

A best friend is like a four leaf clover, hard to find, lucky to have.

Anonymous

Date: ________________

My thoughts for today: ____________________________________

If you don't succeed at first, hide all evidence that you tried.

Anonymous

Date: ________________

My thoughts for today: ____________________________________

If people are talking behind your back, be happy that you are the one in front.

Anonymous

Date: ________________

My thoughts for today: ____________________________________

The secret to happiness is not to do what makes you happy; it's to be happy doing what you're already doing.

Anonymous

Date: ________________

My thoughts for today: ____________________________________

Life isn't measured by the number of breaths you take, but by the number of moments that take your breath away.

Anonymous

Date: ________________

My thoughts for today: ________________________________

The most important thing in life is not knowing everything, it's having the phone number of somebody who does!

Anonymous

Date: ______________

My thoughts for today: ______________________________

Starve your distractions, feed your focus.

Anonymous

Date: ________________

My thoughts for today: ____________________________________

www.ingramcontent.com/pod-product-compliance
Lightning Source LLC
Chambersburg PA
CBHW051932090426
42740CB00032B/2523
* 9 7 8 1 5 9 6 1 1 1 4 8 6 *